Excuse Me While I Live My Life

Words to Reach Your Heart

Clarise Annette Brooks

Excuse Me While I Live My Life:
Words to Reach Your Heart
Copyright © 2021 Clarise Annette Brooks

Visit our website at
www.StillwaterPress.com
for more information.

First Stillwater River Publications Edition

ISBN 978-1-7369767-1-5 (paperback)
ISBN 978-1-955123-92-1 (hardcover)
ISBN 978-1-7369767-0-8 (ebook)

Library of Congress Control Number: 2021923192

1 2 3 4 5 6 7 8 9 10
Written by Clarise Annette Brooks
Cover design by SelfPubBookCovers.com
Interior book design by Matthew St. Jean
Published by Stillwater River Publications,
Pawtucket, Rhode Island, USA

Publisher's Cataloging-In-Publication Data
(Prepared by The Donohue Group, Inc.)

Names: Brooks, Clarise Annette, author.
Title: Excuse me while I live my life :
words to reach your heart / Clarise Annette Brooks.
Description: First Stillwater River Publications edition. |
Pawtucket, RI, USA : Stillwater River Publications, [2021]
Identifiers: ISBN 9781736976715 (paperback) |
ISBN 9781955123921 (hardcover) | ISBN 9781736976708 (ebook)
Subjects: LCSH: Fear--Poetry. | Time--Poetry. |
Nature--Poetry. | Hope--Poetry. | LCGFT: Poetry.
Classification: LCC PS3602.R644252 E98 2021 (print) |
LCC PS3602.R644252 (ebook) | DDC 811/.6--dc23

EXCUSE ME WHILE I LIVE MY LIFE

Contents

Introduction

How do you capture the essence of an emotion, a moment, or a message that you want to share with others in such a way that they can read it within moments, yet remember it forever? You write a poem.

I have loved reading since I was a very small child. I remember how my parents, **Gervais and Judith Brooks**, from the beautiful Caribbean island of **Saint Martin**, worked hard to make sure that my six sisters and I received a great education. Books and libraries were significant parts of our lives. The **Queens Public Library** on 104th Street & 38th Avenue, as well as the **Langston Hughes Community Library & Cultural Center** on Northern Boulevard—both in my hometown of Corona, Queens in New York City— created a love in me that lasts to this day. We went every week. The smell of a new book and the sound of crisp pages turning remain as great sources of comfort to me. In our home, spending time with a good book was always regarded as a great opportunity and a privilege.

The libraries in the schools that I attended—**Our Lady of Sorrows, Flushing High School, Queens College, and the Massachusetts College of Liberal Arts**—were all havens to me. It was fine with me to not be with the cool crowd out on the quad. I *loved* being in the library and having the opportunity to peruse the stacks for my next great find.

And who would think that the greatest of dates would be going to a bookstore? I looked forward to it all week. Hours and hours on a Saturday night amidst the science fiction, the thrillers, the romance, and the poetry sections. Yes, that is what my then boyfriend/now husband—**Alexander Major II**—and I basked in doing on our nights out. It is a beautiful thing to have a handsome man walk up to you and say, "I found this book in that aisle over there. The words on this page remind me so much of you."

We have shared this love of reading with our two precious children—**Alexa Claire** and **Daniel Gervais**—and it does my heart good to see them eagerly awaiting the next part of a book series that they're enraptured in. To listen to your children argue about who is going to get to read a book first, is a pleasurable thing. And when one of the biggest arguments that you have with your teenagers is that they cannot stay up any longer to finish the chapter because you fear that they will be too tired in school the next day, you know that you have passed that bookworm gene on to them.

Now here I present my first book of poetry which was years in the making. It's me scribbling a few lines here and a few stanzas there when I was supposed to be paying attention during various meetings. It's me studying the poetry of the masters so that I could learn how they got it so right. It's me sitting in a writing group learning how to hone my craft. It's my **Alexa** and **Daniel** repeatedly editing my drafts. It's my dearest friend—**Karla Alvarez**—cheering me along because ever since we were very little girls together, she knew that my writing needed to be published. She understood the importance of reminding me to not let life get in the way of making this happen.

I hope this poetry collection will encourage you to live your life the way that you must, instead of how others expect you to. Afterall, it was not being afraid to be the girl-with-the-book, that led me to becoming a lover of words...and that is what brought me to the point where I felt so secure in saying, **Excuse Me While I Live My Life**.

Clarise Annette Brooks

❧ One Life ☙

I recently engaged in a conversation
that focused on this thought:

*What if we had the opportunity to be reborn
knowing everything that we know now?*

Well, I am not sure if I would want to do that,
but the question got me thinking about
important lessons in life that would have been
great to have figured out early on.
There comes a time in our lives when we have to
decide what our "life's mission statement" is.
What do our actions, choices, and statements
say about what our lives mean to us?
Hopefully, you will enjoy the poems in the *One Life*
section of this book and allow them to encourage you
to think about what is going to be held as most
important in your own life so that, in due time,
you can look back and say to yourself,
"Well done."

Excuse Me While I Live My Life

Excuse me, I was walking when you stepped
    right in my stride.
I've got places to go and dreams to live,
    so please let me go by.

> *I know where you are going,*
> *And I even understand,*
> *You've gone ahead and made yourself*
> *Some mighty sturdy plans.*
> *But I've got other thoughts and goals*
> *That I want for you,*
> *So I'll stand right here and block you,*
> *So that you cannot pass on through.*

But who gave you the right to try and do just so?
I am being quite polite, you see, so please just let me go.

> *No, you see, 'cause I want you to do*
> *Just as I want you to.*
> *That's really what will please me,*
> *Even if it doesn't quite please you.*

Why would you stifle my life this way
And disturb my inner peace?
I have my own life to make,
So let me go now, PLEASE.

I won't talk to you, if you do not live just as I say.
Do what I tell you to. You see, I want it just my way.

But that won't make me happy.
It will hurt me really bad.
Do you want me living with regrets?
Do you want me feeling sad?

But just think of what others will say
When they see what I have raised.
I'll be bragged about, and envied,
Admired, and even praised!

Understand, I'm not a "what", I'm a "who" and I love you,
So understand and let me pass...just let me go on through.

Well if you do and you don't succeed,
Don't come running back to me.
I want you just as I want you.
Can't you please just see?

Your words hurt so much. They cut me like a knife.
All the same, I love you, but I choose to live my life.

Then go and don't come back, I don't want to hear from you.
You're not doing what I want...or as I say to do.

Goodbye, but as my life begins...
As I go and make my start,
Just know that you'll forever have a place within my heart.
And I hope that we can sit again and overcome this strife.
But for now please...just excuse me while I live my life.

Fear Is Your Friend

Listen not to those who say,
"Ignore Fear."
They do not understand.
You must realize that Fear is your friend.
But when she comes to visit,
Remember her place in your life:

>Do not place Fear in front of you.
>To do so, is to misunderstand her intention.
>>She will block you from moving forward
>>into the adventures your life may hold.
>>She will be the barrier and you her unintended
>>>captive—
>>unable to move...unable to go forward...trapped.
>>Forever remaining "in your place".
>And your life's closing will be one of regrets and
>wonderings of what *could have* been.

>Do not toss Fear carelessly behind you.
>She resents being ignored.
>>She will shake her head as you fail to give
>>your endeavors the careful thought and planning
>>>that they require.
>>She will stare down at the recklessness caused by
>>your disregard for her cautionary warnings.

And your final reflections will be of torment and
lamentations of how you *could have* triumphed at
the opportunity that once laid before you… and of
berating yourself for so foolishly tossing her to the
side—dishonoring her purpose.

So yes…recognize Fear
and welcome her when she arrives.
Allow her to take her place at your side.
Hold her hand and listen to her as she whispers,
"I am here, my friend, to remind you:
Prepare yourself for this venture.
Learn what you must *before* taking your next step.
Ready yourself for what you must do…and *then*
move forward."
And if you cherish the wisdom of this dear friend,
you will be ready to create the story
that you alone can write.

And even if a chapter goes astray,
you will have the peace of knowing
that it was not due to cowering or to lack of mindful action,
but simply to fate at work.

You will thank her for her time spent with you.
And you will be grateful to her for having afforded you
the peace of your final days.

I Have Lived My Life

When my morning sun rose
I knew early that I had miles to go
Before the set of my day,
So I wasted no time defining my way.

I gathered my strength
And I learned how to stand.
I learned to feed myself
With my own two hands.

And to look at myself
And maintain some self-pride,
I learned to think clearly
And to support the right side.

I did not remain silent
When sound needed to be heard.
I took action fairly...
And I tempered my words.

And I learned to let love in
By opening my heart.
Some whom I loved have remained,
While some had to depart.

But I have always wished well
And held no resentment.
Godspeed to each soul
Was my life testament.

And I danced to the music
And I helped the choir sing.
When I saw joy in your life,
I joined in rejoicing.

And I lent my shoulder
Just for you to cry.
I never judged your feelings
Or made you tell why.

You had your own mind
And your own path to follow.
To have forced you down my road
Would have made my soul shallow.

So I allowed you to feel,
And to seek and explore,
And to find your own joys,
And to open your own doors.

And you thanked me in ways
That showed me you knew
That whatever fair path you took,
My love went with you.

And I never got stuck
In an unmoving rut.
I made changes in my life
And I relied on my gut.

I learned that fear is okay
It even helped keep me smart.
I learned to balance it though
With what I felt in my heart.

Yes, I kept fear in its place
Not in front...but at my side.
I never let it control
What I had to decide.

This was the greatest of gifts
To myself I could give.
It allowed me to shine.
It allowed me to live!!!

And I lived within means.
I'm no bill collector's slave!!!
I kept some stashed on the side
And to some charities I gave.

No, I never got burdened
And bogged down with debt.
I paid every bill.
Heck...that's why I slept!!!

And I learned there was no better place
For keeping it real,
Than to sit with my loved ones
In sharing a meal.

So I'd set about
Creating a sacred space
With my family and friends,
Always first giving grace.

Each voice was heard.
Each one shared a smile—
Our elders and mid-aged
And most especially...each child.

And I never forgot
To say, "Thank you," and "Please."
One simple, "God bless you,"
Upon hearing a sneeze.

A friend or a stranger,
I didn't care who it was—
A woman on the subway
Or a man on the bus.

Just a bit of some love
To always send,
Because each stranger I met
Was a potential new friend.

So, it is okay...
To now to look at my night
And for the moonlight to glow.
Yes, it is okay now...for me to go.

You see, I was given this life
For only me to mold.
And I treasured it so,
For all to behold.

I stayed true to my heart
And whether that was wrong or right,
It allowed me to truly realize...

That no one could have done it—
Lived this life of mine.
They didn't know the song in *my soul*
Or the power of *my mind.*

Because...

When my morning sun rose,
I knew early that I had to define my own way—
And *that* is what gives me this peace
As my sun sets today.

Life Got in the Way

Wait…you mean this is it?
I can't have another day?
There's more that I meant to do,
But life got in the way.

You see, there are some things
That I let wait for another day.
I meant to get right back to them,
But there was always some delay.

And there are friends to call…
So many things I want to say.
I put off reaching out to them,
Because I thought that would be okay.

They did so many nice things for me.
I'm indebted, and I want to repay.
I've always meant to…I swear I did.
But, I put it off 'til another day.

And I meant to tell my loved ones
About how I have always prayed
To say they make me thankful—
Another plan that I've betrayed.

And there was going to be a time
Set aside to just laugh and play.
But I was busy with so many things
And said I'd get to it someday.

And I had planned to relax sometime...
Take a vacation one fine day.
But there were always things to do,
That all kept getting in my way.

And I had sworn to myself,
One day I'll do something *really* brave,
Just step right out of my comfort zone...
But it never went that way.

So, please, if I could have more time,
Even just *one more day*.
I promise that I will live it *so well*
And not let "life" get in the way.

May this soul rest in peace.

Boxed

Did you know your world was open
When you first arrived?
The possibilities were endless,
So many reasons yet to thrive.

But someone said, "Stop now.
Get back inside your box.
Remain where it is known and safe."
That's when your mind began to lock.

You stayed right there and you watched
While others lived out their dreams,
While you believed the lie
That only THEY were born for great things.

And when you questioned, you were told,
"Hush now. Don't talk silly.
That life's not for you or me.
Just strive for normalcy."

So you asked once more and were told again,
"Stop talkin' like a fool.
You can't do those kinds of things.
That ain't for me or you."

So there you stayed and you remained
Believing the common lie,
That keeps you locked inside your box—
That's now locked from the inside.

I Looked Around and Realized

I looked around and realized
That years had come and gone.
I'd awoken from the dreams I had...
Countless feats yet to be done.
When I was young,
I knew that I would do something so great.
I just saw within my mind that this would be my fate.

But I put things off, you see, for another time.
Waiting for the "just right" moment
Seemed like it'd be just fine.

And now I've come to realize that I can no longer wait.
Please somebody...anybody,
Tell me it's not too late.

The Trade

She said she dreads her birthday.
Such a foolish thing to say.

She is here.
She has the power to be.
She IS!!!

Would she prefer that she is not?
And what is it she cries over...a spot?
A wrinkle? An ache?
A strand of hair that is now gray?

This is what causes her such strife?
The signs of longevity within her life?

She is strong!!!
Yet foolish worries make her spirit become frayed!
I knew so many who would have loved...
the chance to trade.

✢ *Me* ✣

"Me". That word is thrown around so often.
I am wondering if anyone ever stops to define
what it really means.

Think about it:
If every single person in this world stopped
to define that word, there would be a multitude of
responses. And just what exactly would each of these
responses be based upon? When you say the word "Me"
what definition comes to your mind and how do you
make the awareness of your "Me" known to others?
What exactly does your "Me" stand for?

Hate, Venture Not

Hate, venture not toward my soul
For you will not prosper there.
Bring not to me, thy deadly sins—
Those friends you hold so dear.

For peace of mind and care of soul
There is a lesson I have learned.
It is: Make no room within my heart
For the temptations of this world.

So swarm around me if you must,
Run upon land and sea,
But you waste your time, if you believe
You will ever have hold of me.

The Lesson

 I realize that it is time, you see
To teach you how to treat me.
Not as *you* want, but as *I* say.
So get this lesson down today.

Regardless of the mood *you're* in,
If worries are makin' *your* head spin,
Whether your mood is high or low,
Don't lash out at me for your own ego.

You might be stressed and want your say.
I know at times it gets that way.
But watch how you come to me and talk,
'Cause, trust me, I can turn and walk.

I won't engage or act in kind...
Won't leave that kind of rep behind.
I'll stay respectful, but I will turn to you
And tell you just a thing or two.

Like get yourself together, friend,
Before you speak to me again.
Catch yourself. Regain control.
Calm your mind and ease your soul.

I will listen. I'll be here.
Do not think that I don't care.
What you're feeling truly matters,
So I'll try to give you helpful answers.

So come now...
I believe that we can start anew.
Tell me please,
How do you do?

My Soul Is Planted

In certain ways I don't mind floating
Just like the leaves in fall.
In other ways, I will not acquiesce.
No sir, not at all.

You see on certain things, I can bend
Without feeling at all dismantled.

But...

On things that matter most to me,
On these, my soul is planted.

Some say that I am calm.
They even say I can seem cool.
I never scream and get all loud
Or act like some damned fool.

I will not disarray myself.
You won't see me getting frantic.
Because, I'm telling you my dear,
This soul of mine is planted.

Now I enjoy my fun
And my little sip at happy time.
I don't worry 'bout trends or if I'm thin,
Because I feel just fine.

I dress up in my duds
And my fine hat that I wear slanted.
And I'm fine with whoever looks at me,
Because my soul is planted.

I respect that you have your ways.
I'm not asking you to change.
You like your things. This I acknowledge,
Even if I find them strange.

And if you're with me, understand this:
Don't approach me heavy handed.
I'll speak up for myself. I know who I am,
Because my soul is planted.

We can still talk and share our thoughts.
We can even be real candid.
Just remember—
I ain't tryin' to change you and you won't change me,
Because...my soul is planted.

Begin with Me

There was no particular reason,
No special holiday or season.
I just awoke and as I lay,
I heard my gentle spirit say,

"Please, no routines today.
For once, just go a different way.
Please...just give us this one day."

Now I'd heard that voice several times before,
But I had always chosen to ignore.
Responsibilities overruled!!!
Too many things to always do.
Too many people to answer to.
If *I* wasn't there, what would they do?

But today, for some reason...I don't even know why,
I heard my spirit and finally I obliged.

So I called in...with a feeling of dread.
"OK. Goodbye,"
Is all they said.
So I responded, "OK,"
And I went ahead.

No real plans. Just headed out.
I walked around and ventured about.
A cup of coffee with a fancy name.
A long walk down that pretty lane.
Bought a scarf I didn't need.
It was green...and nice, indeed.
I tossed it on and moved along,
Then started humming some old song.
I didn't even know the name.
'Just popped itself into my brain.

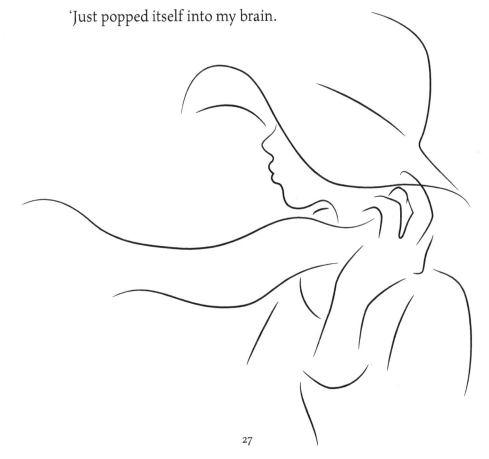

And I must have hummed for quite a while
'Cause people looked at me and smiled.
Now usually, I am quite shy.
But today...I smiled back and then waved, "Hi."

I walked along my little stroll,
Loosening typical self-control.
I embraced all that I saw in this world,
Like I hadn't done since I was a girl.

Yes, I took it in and absorbed it all
And by the time that dark began to fall,
I knew that something had to give
If I was *truly* going to live,
And love, and laugh, and lift my heart.
And today—today would finally be the start.

Then I stopped for a moment and I thought:
When did we become so overwrought?
Who said to have success that we should
Make stressful ways our greater good?

Am I keeping up?
Am I doing okay?
Why do we live
By what others say?

'Cause it's a race.
Until we die
So shut up. Don't think.
Do not ask, "Why?"

We've responsibilities, okay, yes.
We have our jobs and days of stress.
And *things* and *stuff* to all sort out
That pressure us so, and leave us in doubt.
We've got to do them, yes I see...
But today it became quite clear to me:

You see, my spirit, she made me listen today
To what, for so long, she'd been trying to say.
But sometimes my head is too darned hard,
And I find it difficult to lower my guard.
I just couldn't be "Supershe" for this 24.
I needed something, just a little bit more.
I needed time. I needed air.
I needed to just...just be here.
With no clocking in and no deadlines.
I needed to simply clear my mind.

She said:
    "Take care of what you have to, Dear
    But when I speak, please stop and hear.
    When I'm telling you to take a break,
    Just listen please, for goodness' sake.

Yes, live responsibly and keep your word.
Don't let your duties go deferred.
Just make it a point to let in the joy.
Because you are worthy...you are ROYAL!!!

You're not in this world to only pass a test,
To be filled with worries or consumed in stress.
And Darling...never forget...
That you are truly so very blessed.
And remember, you have the power to be
The face of peace that others see."

And so I heard,
And I cherished each word,
And by nightfall,
I had embraced it all.

And tomorrow, I will step back into "my role,"
But...I think I will do so with a bit more soul.
I'll take a break and maybe even a walk.
I'll stop by someone's desk to talk.
I'll remember to smile a wee bit more,
Because life needn't be such an awful bore.
I can crack my day open and make it more bright
And be that someone who adds a little more light

To the gloomy, moody, draggy day,
Because it doesn't need to be that way.
Amongst all of the noise and the deadlines and the chatter,
I can remind those I am with that they matter.
We're not just a bunch who gather for eight hours
To simply perform duties and to be devoured
By rules and demands by those who hold power.

And I say,
"Thank you, my spirit, for making me see
That the goodness you gave is not only for me.
If I take care of me, I can appreciate others,
And be kinder and gentler to my sisters and brothers.
Spirit...now I can say that I see your plan.
I get it now...I understand.
If I want more joy to be felt, and heard, and seen.
I must *always* first, begin with me."

Climb

When I started my ascent,
First climbing one rung, then two,
You tossed dirt down on my face
And you thought that I'd be through.

But I brushed it off and I kept on
Climbing to three, then four.
And you shook the ground so very hard
Thinking I'd brave it no more.

But I held on tight and I kept on
Climbing to five, then six.
You blew hot wind down and I will admit
It burned...but I held my grip.

I looked ahead...almost there
Climbing to seven, then eight.
And you stomped with a fury that was
so great...
So filled to the brim you were with hate.

But I did it! I finally did it!
Reaching to nine and then ten.
So remember our little story
And never doubt upon me again!

If I Cease to Seize This Moment

If I cease to seize this moment,
I will dwell within lament.
I will live with self-chastisement
And feelings of regret.

If I cease to seize this moment,
All the plans inside my mind
Will begin to minimize,
And then be left behind.

If I cease to seize this moment,
Then I will never know
How the greatness I once sought,
Could have been nurtured and well sown.

And if I cease to seize this moment,
I will never see,
The person that I always knew
I had the power to be.

I Take Time in the Morning

I take time in the morning,
Time that is just for me.
I do this, you see, for my sanity.

I know what is coming,
So I cannot neglect,
To take this time each morning to stop and to reflect.

It's a habit of sorrow
To begrudge a brand new day.
I will not allow that kind of thinking to become my way.

So I will not whine
And I will not moan.
And I *refuse* to greet the day by reaching for my phone.

'Cause I don't need someone's gossip
Or some hysterical headlines.
Instead, I *choose* to create a sense of peace within my mind.

So I will bask in my moment
And first clear my own head...
Just take a moment to appreciate my life's glories instead.

I said, I will take my moment
To just grab hold.
A moment, as they say, to first restoreth my soul.

And when I am done
And I am feeling my own steady—
I will then get up and say, "Hey new day, I'm ready."

My Past Is Not Untouched

You made an error that impacted me.
I feel quite cross with you.
Though my first thought is to seek revenge,
I know first what I must do:

    I have first to revisit my own life
    Filled with its own travails—
    Moments when I meant to do well,
    But instead fell short and failed.
    Moments when I did not mean harm,
    But still, I inflicted pain.
    You see, my past is not untouched,
    For it bares its own faults and stains.

And once done with my own reflection
Ready to embrace our difficult talk,
I am able to come from a place
Of someone who has walked your walk.
For I know the seat where you now sit,
Because it is a place where I once lived.
It is for this reason I can truly say,
I understand and I forgive.

A Little Jaunt

Can I step out and look about?
Can I discover what's around?
Can I find what's out there just for me?
Can I just take a little peek and see?

Because I am feeling a wee bit bored—
Like I need time to stretch and soar.
I'm feeling like I need to sing
And do a few sweet joyful things.

I want some days with pretty sights
Along with warm and lingering nights.
I want less of the same-old-same,
And for a while, to not hear everybody calling my name!

So I'll be off for a little bit
To refill and rekindle my ole spirit.
Then I'll be back and I'll be fine.
But for now...I'm just gonna take some time.

Home

Despite what happens
   in this world,
   at work,
   in the street,
In places where my power to make a difference
   may seem weak,

When I enter my home...
When my feet step firmly through this door...
When I walk into this place I have worked so hard for...

There will be tranquility
In this haven for my family.
It is our sacred sanctuary.

And though my home may seem quite small,
It is filled with kindness for one and all.

It is a place where there will be calm.
There is a love here that will keep you warm.
And I will always do my very best
To make your time here be truly blessed.

So wrap yourself in the peace that is here.
Consume the goodness that is shared.
And when it comes time for you to leave,
Won't you please...
Spread that goodness around out there.

Yes, the love that dwells here is yours to take.
Let this be the difference that I can make.

❯❯ *You* ❮❮

The impact that you have on others can be transformative.
The time you spend with others—whether long or short—
is time when the words that you choose to share
and the actions that you choose to take
can have a lasting effect on the life of another person.
How do you approach others? Regard others? Treat others?
What part of you do you leave with them
well after you have left them?

This Way, That Way

You say to live life this way,
But then you live yours that way.

You claim that what you say is right,
But I am keeping you in sight.

And what I see just kinda trips
With what keeps comin' from your lips.

You're always there to say a mouthful,
But your actions are leaving me quite doubtful.

So think for just a moment or two
Before tryin' to tell me just what to do.

Connect your actions to your message,
'Cause it will help to improve your image.

The Shout and Then the Whisper

When you had words of cruelty
Of blame and even scorn,
You did not think to hesitate
To shout them loud and strong.

It did not even matter
That there were others so nearby.
You bellowed like you enjoyed it,
Even as you saw me cry.

But then you finally realized
The full story through and through.
You saw the blame fell not with me,
You saw it fell with you.

Then you smiled and even laughed.
You said, "Ain't no need to worry."
You then tried to do nice things for me
As you lamely whispered, "Sorry."

Notice, please, if you will,
Your insults come through in shouts.
But why is it *big ole brave one*
That your apology is just whispered out?

Surprises

Do you remember
the times when you would meet me by surprise
simply because I was on your mind,
and we walked for hours
taking the long way on purpose?
And when we got there,
we sat
sometimes talking...and...sometimes not.

Of gifts and trinkets and the rest,
I like these surprises best.

I Walk So Proudly With You

I walk so proudly with you
Because of who you are.
It matters not who looks upon us
As we walk this journey far,
Because you are good and you are righteous
And you are proud and you are strong
And your integrity sustains you throughout every day
   so long.

So let others look upon us
And see just who we are,
Because you are mine and I adore you.
So come...let's journey on.

You Have Lived the Miracles

You have lived the miracles.
You are a wonder.
You have done glorious things.

No, it is not blasphemous to say so.
For if we do not learn them, then let them guide us,
Then what good are all the learnings of the gospels?

From the most meager of moments,
You have created sweetness.
When others would have thought,
"We have run dry. It is all lost."
It was you who found a way to create a joy
From seemingly nothing.
It was you who created what quenched
The spiritual parchedness that others
Had resolved themselves too.

And when most had no hope left in one child,
You listened to him, comforted him.
You cooled the fever of despair
That was burning his soul,
And making him want to be no more.
There are many ways to ail, besides the pains of the flesh,
Just as there are many ways to heal.

It was you who touched his soul and mended it
When others had surrendered him
To the cause of affliction that had been consuming his life.

And to the one who was paralyzed with grief
So sorrowful and unable to stand—inconsolable,
You listened with love, while others ran from the despair
And from the grief that immobilized him.
Others were concerned first and only with
Their own discomfort.
So they left.
But you heard and you aided,
Unfrightened by another's tears...
Realizing that they are simply
The natural release of sorrow
That must be shed before one can stand again
    and carry on.

And when it seemed like there was not enough
For even us to eat,
You managed not only for your own home,
But also for those who came to our door.
Over time, you have welcomed and fed the masses.
Providing for all, from so little.
This is the gift of your hands
And the generosity of your heart.

And when some needed rescuing...no matter how afar,
You were there in the dark and in the rain...on your way.
The storm did not deter you.
They feared you would not make it and that
They would drown in desperation,
But there you were...triumphant,
Through the downpour.
A rescue...a comfort to those who needed you.

And when some could not see
Through the blindness of confusion—
Preferring to spew hateful words and insults
Instead of understanding another's vantage,
You remained steadfast, calm.
You helped them to see clarity.
No judging...just listening.
You were the voice of reason that could not be denied.
You helped them to see sides beyond their own and to
    seek to understand.

And to those who had totally given up—
Whose souls had been left for dead,
You helped them to see reason to look for tomorrow,
And to relight their lives.
You knew they had so much more to offer,
Even when they could not see it themselves.

And they are here now—rekindled and triumphant—
Because of your belief in them
And because you helped them discover that there are
    days yet worth living.

You chose to not only hear the words from
    The Good Book,
But to live them.
What are they for, if not to be brought to life in
    common day?

But there will be no gospels written of you.
There will be no palms waving.
Your glory is in the love we have for you.
You are the grace of the now.
For you have learned from His steps.
For you have lived the miracles.

You Saw It Within Me

What is it you saw that I did not
When I was still so frightened and distraught?

Did you notice a sign behind me
That my own eyes could not see?
Did someone whisper to you
That my best was yet to be?

I did not see the signage.
I only saw the dark.
I heard no words of comfort.
My soul was cold and stark.

But you told me that was not my end.
You spoke of my tomorrows.
You spoke of me succeeding
As I spiraled in my sorrows.

You saw it within me,
And now it has come to be.
How can I ever thank you
For believing so in me?

Time, Nature & Us

We are given gifts from nature that can be healing to us.
We can receive this healing if we just stay still
long enough to welcome it.

The Wind Went Wild

The wind went wild one Wednesday morn,
and blew my pain away.

Yes, the wind went wild one Wednesday morn,
and now I'm not the same.

I was holding on to worries and stress
and things I can't control

But then the wind went by that Wednesday morn
and said, "Chile, just let it go."

Sunday Morn

What is it about a Sunday morn?
Of the seven days, it stands quite alone.

The same number of hours,
The same number of minutes...
But there's a peace that exists
So deeply within it.

Five days of work, five days to rush,
And one day just to clean—
Errands completed on the eve,
Then...finally...the day to breathe.

It begins from the moment you open your eyes
And take your first look upon the grand morning sky.
It is then that a calm is offered to you,
And it is up to you to choose what to do.

Whether you choose to use this day to pray
Or to call an old friend to simply say,
"How are you doing? How is your day?
Just want you to know that I hope you're ok.
That's the only reason that I called you today."

Perhaps it's simply for taking a rest
After changing out of your Sunday best.
Or for family and loved ones and gatherings,
And cooking and talking and long lingering meals.

What is it about a Sunday morn,
That brings that feeling that's felt the day long?
Perhaps, it's not even to be understood.
Perhaps, I'll accept that it just makes me feel good.

I Was There When the Rain Began to Fall

The others do not understand.
The raindrops are solace for our souls.
The rhythm lulls us into a calmer state.
They refresh us.

The darkening of the sky prepares you for them.
It tells you, "Rest for a moment. Relax. Calm yourself.
I am preparing you for a moment of comfort."

The drivers slow down.
If they choose, they can enjoy the solace.
No honking. No radio.
Just the rhythm of the drops upon their car tops.

The walkers start to scurry with their heads down.
Why?
Will they get less wet if they go fast?
Once you are totally wet, can you get less wet?
So why the rushed steps?
Just walk.

We are bathing together in His shower upon us.
It is okay.
Smile at wet tendrils. They're funny.
Slide them from your eyes.
Look up.

You already know the ground is wet,
So look up at the rain as it greets you.
Yes, it is beautiful.

And you can even do it,
Because you know that you want to.
It's not just for the child you once were.
So go ahead.
Jump in.
Splash!

It's a gift.
Welcome it.
Then you can earn the chance to say,
"I was there when the rain began to fall.
You missed it.
That is all."

The Tree in My Hometown Park

There's a tree in my hometown park.
I did not have my own backyard, you see.
But she was mine all the same,
Standing tall and majestically.

And she loved me. I know she did.
She grew a special branch just for me.
It reached strong for me to sit upon.
Quite sturdy, yes indeed.

And when I ran away from home
For an hour or two or three,
I knew just where to go.
She was waiting there for me.

One day I brought a friend
To come and climb with me.
And we talked and laughed enjoying
Our tree party of just three.

It's hard for me to climb now.
I've changed, but not my tree.
It's been decades and I miss her.
Does she still remember me?

She Is a River

She is a river,
Deep and flowing,
Cool and refreshing.
Go within her and she will sway you.
Lay upon her and she will uphold you.
But lay right, or she will consume you.

She runs far,
Yet she is there for you.
Let her carry you. She will move you forward.
Let her wet you. She will refresh you.
But treat her right, or she will parch.

She is a river.
Consider her depths
Admire her flow.
Respect her strength.
But mind your row.

Please Understand

It is hard to see situations from another person's view. We may hear their stories and explanations, but not fully "get it". We're left wondering, "What are they complaining about?" Perhaps some will never understand the vantage of others, but that does not make their perspectives any less valid.

You Did Not Know

I cannot blame you
because you did not know.
You see,
you thought that you were speaking
only to me.

You did not know
That I am made of all the ones who came before me,

Those who were forced to act weak;
      therefore, you see, I must speak.
Those who were beaten and took the fall;
      therefore, I am charged to always stand tall.
Those whose babies were stolen or slaughtered;
      so I embrace and fight
      for my sons and my daughters.
Those silenced and stripped of their voices;
      therefore, I cherish the right for my choices.
Those who were denied an education;
      I am a teacher, I teach the nation.
Those whose days were of pure torment;
      So I stand for them now and I represent.

I will not let them down.

So now you know.

Be Careful Where You Spend

Ohhhhh, be careful where you spend now.
Some places loooooooove your money,
But they don't love you!
Sit back now and let me tell you some truth!!!

You go to that store
All the way across town,
And the second you enter,
They start following you around.

All you want is to go in,
Get what you want and then leave.
But they start treating you
As if you're some sort of a thief.

You say you're looking for that.
They say, "Just get this!"
You say, "Please listen to me.
I'm not in here tryin' to be dissed."

When you find what you want
And you're finally ready to pay,
They then have the nerve
To stand there and say,

"Oh it's not the right price
It was marked much too low,
So I charged you a bit higher.
Here. Now take it and go."

You say, "Wait!!! You did what???
You just overcharged my card?
You can't demand more.
That's my cash. I work hard!!!"

"If you want it, you pay.
It is not a big deal.
To charge you less,
Would be like letting you steal."

"Do you think I am crazy?
The mistake is not mine.
I'm not going to stand here,
While you rob me blind."

"If you don't like it, then leave.
Get away from this store.
Shop somewhere else.
Don't come here no more."

"First give me my money.
Refund it now, if you please.
Return every penny,
And then I will leave!"

> *"Here take your money,*
> *We don't care about you.*
> *If you come back here again,*
> *We'll call the cops on you."*

So you gather yourself,
And as you step outside,
Someone who looks like you,
Takes a step inside.

You take a peek through the window
And cannot help but frown;
As you look inside and see,
That they're following her around.

They Dreamt

They dreamt those days would become outdated—
Moments from history.
But it seems they never went away.
They're just shrouded in mystery.

The methods have changed,
But the results are the same.
Haters use new ploys, but it's the same old game.
Families lay broken and are left crying.
Because, you see, their loved ones are dying.

And what is this for? How did it begin?
Just a difference in the shading of our skin?
Help me please. I just do not understand.
Is there any woman, is there any man,
Who can explain the root, the cause, the hate?
'Cause by my soul I swear, peace can no longer wait.

Dreams of You

When you look back at us and wonder
How we dealt with our dim plight,
During our days of pain and anguish
And night hours brimmed with fright.

When you ponder how we sustained it
For what was our eternity,
How we toiled each day upon this earth,
Denied humanity.

Remember that our one gleam of light—
The only hope worth holding onto—
Were not of dreams that were for ourselves,
We carried on for dreams of you.

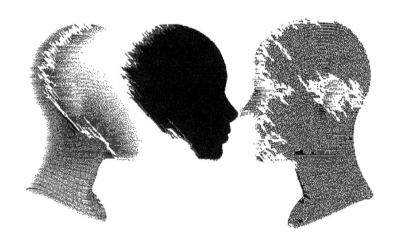

When I Learn of My People

When I learn of my people,
I do not bow my head,
I do not feel one bit of shame,
I feel no sense of dread.

When I learn of my people,
I grow in resiliency,
Empowered by the strength they gave me.
It forms my identity.

When I learn of my people,
I know how I must live.
I am the embodiment of their dreams.
They gave all that they could give.

And when I learn of my people,
It gives me such great pride,
To know *whatever* may come my way,
The blood runs through me
      to survive.

Great for All...Finally

I had a philosophical chat
That had no harm intended,
But he stopped speaking to me
By the time that chat had ended.

It took a moment to understand
What ticked him off just so,
But then he turned, and he looked back,
And said to me, "Just go!
If you don't like this land of ours
Then hop a boat or plane.
I'm sick of all you people
Who want to just complain."

And I said, "Hey, now wait a minute
It's not from hate that I spoke.
When I say we need to work on things,
I say it 'cause I'm woke.
You see, I'm not the kind of person
To smile and keep pretending,
Especially when there are situations
That need some real amending.

Cause just yelling, 'Love it or leave it'
Is the easy thing to say,
But because I am strong, you see,
I'll find another way.
I'll take the jibes
And bare the yells.
I'll be chastised
And I'll catch the hell.

Because you see I know what we can be.
So by my soul, I will not be done
'Til we hear from not just the few,
But from the voices of EVERYONE.

And you, my friend,
May not understand
Because your walk has been different
Upon this land.

So trust me,
You would be surprised,
If you walked my walk
And saw through my eyes.

Yes, if you could only live
In a life that is "not the same"
Then you would share my vision
And you would not give me blame.

And it's *because* I love it, that I *will not* leave it.
I'll work to make it for you *and* me.
That's right! We *can* make our country great
But great for ALL...**FINALLY**.

✤ *Hope* ✤

Hope is the thing that keeps us going
when it becomes difficult, or even unbearable,
to linger in our current state.
Believing—truly believing—that despite
what our current situation is,
there is a way that we can get out of it,
that we can truly improve it,
and that the power is truly within us to do so,
is what true hope really is.
Hope is not a wish.
A wish is, "Perhaps something will happen,"
but hope is, "I see it and I can make it happen."

Cashless

My pockets are empty,
But my mind is full.
I'm gonna create something beautiful.

It ain't fun
Being the only one who's broke,
But that's gonna change, 'cause I tell ya I'm woke.

And when I do,
I will finally be
Livin' a bit easier with a bit of some green.

But I won't get stupid.
I swear that y'all,
'Cause what's worse than cashless, is losing it all.

So watch me.
Just see the steps that I'm making,
'Cause success for who wants it, is there for the taking.

These Fleeting Moments

These fleeting moments
of worry and strife
will not be allowed to define my life.

Although it now feels
like countless tomorrows
will be drowned within these tremendous sorrows,

I will remain steadfast
during this temporary state.
It is I alone...who will design my fate.

And although this time
brings such worry and pain,
I know that enduring it will not be in vain.

For I will walk through it
one step at a time
to design the life that is rightfully mine.

And despite...that in this moment...
there is so much going wrong,
I will remain whole and I will emerge strong.

In Times of Trouble

It is in times of trouble, when you're feeling most alone,
That a terror seems to strike and it can cut to the bone.
Your heart feels unsettled, your soul shaken within.
You stare at the simplest task, with no idea where to begin.

And even when you lay still, you are unable to rest,
So consumed and overwhelmed with this feeling of stress.
You don't know where to turn,
And have no clue where to go.
You wonder if you'll recover from feeling so low.

And it may seem to come from nowhere.
It can strike us unaware.
It brings a frightening feeling,
Of paralyzing despair.
It is at this moment that we tell the greatest lie,
Because when asked how we're feeling, we force a smile
    and say, "Fine."

But please...please remember, and know this is true,
You aren't the only person that this angst happens to.
Every girl, every boy, every woman, every man
Have had moments of this dread
That we don't fully understand.

So we must talk about it—
Stop hiding it in shame.
Come to the understanding
That you are not to blame.

It's emotional care that we must start to seek
And doing so DOES NOT mean that you are weak!
In fact, it is helpful in becoming so much stronger.
Let not the stigma hold us back any longer.

If you broke a bone or got hurt somehow,
You'd simply scream, "Please, get me help now!"
So why then dwell within emotional strife,
When doing so harms you...and can cost you your life?

So breathe, my friend, breathe. Take it in and let it out.
Realize, dear one, that this is what life's sometimes about.
There'll be more times of trouble and feelings unnamed.
To allow them to diminish you, would be such a shame.

We are all in it my dear, every one of us.
We all have troubled feelings...even those "not discussed".
So let us live as full beings as we exist and as we feel.
For we are only human and THAT is what keeps us real.

In Just One Year

In just one year...
I can be in such a different place
One that I can finally embrace.

I need to change some things around,
ease my soul and remain calm...
make my life a bit more sound.

No more of the chaos that has become my norm.
I decree the release of my internal storm.

I need to assess and to re-arrange.
I need to take hold and to make this change.

I acknowledge the steps I have made that were wrong
And I accept now the path that will help me grow strong.

As I write my new plan, I will mark this day,
As the moment in time to develop new ways.

The number 180 is a transformative one.
It's the one that I look for to guide me along.
The first step in my journey has now just begun.
I'll look back in a year at the work I have done,
And admire the person I will have become.

Our Vision Boards

Our vision boards are more, you see,
Then hopes-to-be and fantasies.
They're for envisioning goals that can someday be,
Then planning for them carefully.

These scraps of paper all about
Remind us to let go of doubt.
When all laid out, they seem to shout,
"Build your dreams and live them out!"

Friends are near and encouraging.
There are no words disparaging.
We laugh and joke and even sing.
During this sacred gathering.

I am for them. They are for me.
There's a sense of spirituality.
'Cause sharing dreams is not easy.
It's displaying our vulnerability.

So here we are with scraps and dreams,
Building more than hopes and fantasies.
Our vision boards are built, you see
To plan what our lives will someday be.

To Stand in Front

Were certain people born to lead?
What makes some say, "Yes," at the moment of need?
What sacrifices do they make for accepting the challenge?

There's a Calling

There's a calling that only few can hear.
For a path that may yet seem unclear.
It's to those who have the strength to say.
"I accept the charge. I'll lead the way."

And those few who hear and heed the call
Are the ones whose names are said by all.
For it is not a mystery.
That those who heed the call, make history.

And it's not about them.
It's about the deed.
They saw the problem
And they met the need.

And it's not for all.
It's just for the few.
Do you hear the calling?
Is it calling you?

I Declare and I Decree

I declare and I decree:
That Your will begin with me.

I cry out to thee, Dear One,
Let Thy manifest be done.

Let it start this moment now.
I'll do Thy deed, just show me how.

Let me stand when I am weak.
Let me speak when I am shy.
Let me lead, when I'd rather follow.
Let me keep in mind the why.

Let it guide me every day
In what I do and what I say.
Yes, I declare and I decree
That Thy will be done through me.

Stepping Up

Someone has to do it,
So I am stepping up.
The flame inside me has been lit.
My engine's all revved up.

There'll be bumps along the road,
But they won't mess me up.
And there'll be those who tell me, "No,"
And try to make it all go bust.

It's a scary thing to do—
This thing is called stepping up.
'Cause some don't wanna make a change,
They're like hinges full of rust.

Let's let go of the same-ole-same.
No more settling. Start to strut.
Come on, let's raise the bar.
It's time to step our game on up.

'Cause we *can* enact the vision.
Let's hold our expectations up.
Come on and join this journey,
'Cause we've gotta shake things up.

The Disruptor

They call me "The Disruptor".
They say I'm such a pain.
'Cause I won't allow their hurtful ways
To harm someone once again.

They say live within the written laws,
But what if those laws are wrong?
They say, "Well that's just how it is,"
But I am sick of that old song.

So they call me "The Disruptor"
And that's okay with me.
I'd rather disrupt the wrongs in life
And fight for liberty.

Yes, I'll go down as "The Disruptor"
I'm up for a good ole fight.
And I'll keep fighting every day and night
For what I know is right.

Our Journey Is Still Long

Rest for just a moment
Beneath the rays of the bright sun,
Let them energize your spirit
For work yet to be done.

Our cause is so very great
The need is truly vast,
So hold tightly to those rays.
Let the energy they give you last.

Now come along, fellow warriors,
We must now carry on.
There is much that lays before us.
For our journey is still long.

This One & That One

This one's a leader.

        We will have to keep her.

That one's a boss.

        That's truly such a loss!

This one shares.

        That means she cares.

That one just talks.

        Then alone she will walk.

This one can discuss.

        She is building trust.

That one just yells.

        She's just raising hell.

This one speaks straight.

        Great way to communicate.

That one doublespeaks.

        That means she is weak.

This one says, "Ours."

        She knows to share the power.

That one just blames.

        She likes causing shame.

This one builds community.

        She creates a sense of unity.

That one works top down.

        Her folks won't stick around.

This one shares the plan.

        So all can understand.

That one likes to scare.

                    Oh, that's not fair.

This one builds tomorrows.

                    Then her team will always follow.

That one dwells on the past.

                    Then she will not last.

This one's plan sustains.

                    That will allow for great gains.

That one hears only her own voice.

                    So her team lacks choice.

This one's a leader.

                    We will definitely have to keep her.

That one's a boss.

                    Then she has already lost.

The Leadership Business

It looks like respect. It looks like power.
It looks like progress is made each hour.
It looks impressive and worthy of praise.
It looks like your status has been firmly raised.

It looks like the answers are always known.
It looks like the wisdom has been firmly grown.
It looks like always knowing the way.
It looks like always having the right words to say.

It looks like insults never ever matter.
It looks like thoughts are never ever scattered.
It looks like always knowing just what to do...
But don't believe for a moment that this is true.

That is what it *looks like* when you erroneously read
The lives of those in positions,
Where they're required to lead.
Yes—your thoughts would be terribly belied,
If you knew a *caring* leader from the inside.

It's pressure and worry and moments of doubt.
It's countless things to always figure out.
It's feeling like sometimes they want to tear you apart
When they speak of you as if you do not have a heart.

It's knowing that before the setting of the sun
That important projects MUST get done.
It's pressure and worry and not always having assistance...
This is the reality of the leadership business.

It's sacrifice, uneasiness, and always taking the blame.
All while keeping the strength to remain in the game.
It's having what's needed to grow that position.
It's remaining focused on what you know is the mission.

It's celebrating the wins, and it's facing the hardships.
It's making each team member feel a sense of ownership,
It's taking a moment to say, "Thanks for all that you do,"
Even though others forget to say that to you.

It's working late hours when you'd rather go home.
It's staying up late and feeling alone.
It's being at meetings when you'd rather be elsewhere.
It's finding the ways to remind your loved ones you care.

And when you'd prefer a quiet moment to rest,
It's time for family moments and trying your best
To make time for loved ones though you're feeling so tired.
Time now for personal commitments that you know
    are required.

So remember that leadership is a tough role to own.
It can leave you broken and hurt to the bone.
Think carefully before you step up to that plate.
Can you handle the burden? Can you carry the weight?

Can you still provide the answer
To your own personal "why"?
Can that provide you with the strength
That you need to get by?
Is it enough to sustain you and to keep you strong,
As you tread down the road the leadership business is on?

Voice

What is your true voice?
Is it truly yours or has someone else
taken ownership of it?
What does your voice stand for?
What are you without it?

Voice

Did you know,
that each part of you,
each and every solitary part,
both the seen,
and the unseen,
relies upon your voice

—spoken, written, or displayed—

to be known
when it needs to be known?

Do not disappoint.

If I Stay Silent

If I stay silent
When Thy will must be done,
Then truly
I am the guilty one.

For the assailant has already
Lost his soul,
No longer seeing his victim
As one who is whole.

For whatever malady
Has captured his mind,
He is lost forever
And to justice, he is blind.

But I am here
And I can share
The words of justice
That all need to hear.

And if I fail
To share my voice
Can I accept the consequence
Of my choice?

So give me the strength
And the fortitude,
To do what Thy will
Calls me to do.

Intuition

Why have you thrown away your most precious gift?
What will you use to guard yourself now?
She knows you better than you do.
She even knows that part of you that you tucked away
    to hide from yourself.
Without her, you will fall for the whims of others.
Please go find her and bring her back.
When there is something to decide,
It is she who must dig in-tu-it with you.
Go back and get her.
Hold her tight.

Me, Before It Happened

I heard that you have been wondering
Why I am not always smiling
And why I am not always ready to jump in on the fun.

I heard what you have been asking about me,
"Why can't *that one* just be more like the others?"
"Why can't *that one* just act in way that is more pleasant
    for us?"

It's not like I don't want to be.
It's just that I no longer know how to be.

It's too bad that you did not know me...
    before it happened.

Say Nothing

Why are we supposed to say nothing?
Is the greater harm, that people will know
what she or he truly is?
what she or he truly does...
when nobody else is looking?
Will it disrupt the ebb and flow?

Why are they more happy
if we just stay in our room...
Silent...
not letting out the words that will
forever change things?

"Just go away
and never say."

But when decades have passed
and we've gained the strength
to explode,
why do they say,

"Oh no...
that was too long ago.
You're wrong to not just let it go.
If you were going to wait this long,
you should have just...
said nothing."

On a Pedestal High

You hold me on a pedestal high
But if you saw how oft I cry
Desperately trying to just get by,
You'd wonder then and ask me, "Why?"

Why do you act so bold
When there's so much hurt within your soul?
Why be this way, from youth to old?
Why, by fear and sorrow, are you controlled?

And I would listen and then I'd say,
That I was taught to act this way.
For each and every single day,
I must, you see, tuck my true voice away.

The Storm Inside Sits Quietly

There's a storm that brews within me
And it unsettles me so.

I want to be that deep one who others stop to listen to,
Like thunder.
But I was taught to be quiet
Because that's what the nice girls do.
This way everyone just compliments you
Because nobody has anything to
Insult us for,
Criticize us for,
Or talk about us for…
Except to say,
"She's such a nice quiet girl."

But I want them to know that I think...
Even if I am not yet sure of *what* I think.
I know what *you* think...
I know what *they* think...
But I don't know yet what I *should* think
And I worry that when I do,
It might make someone angry
And they will question me
Or YELL at me,
And I won't be able to respond
As quickly as they do,
Or as loudly as they can,
Or sound as smart as they can make themselves sound
    (even if they are faking).
And I will then *have to* be quiet again.

And then they won't look at me the same anymore,
Because I will no longer be someone who is just quiet.
I would then be someone who is just best when quiet.
So I just sit here quietly.

❧ *Words Remain* ❧

Some may believe that weapons
are the most powerful forces in our world,
but it is our thoughts and our words
that drive us to either embrace one another
or to use weapons against each other.
Words reflect our thoughts, express our beliefs,
and cast light upon our character.
The words that you choose to share
can never be erased.
One simple sentence can be cherished
forever in one's heart or it can cause
eternal torment of one's spirit.
The power of words is the greatest
of powers that we have.

Words Never Ever Go Away

I'd like to give you a gift today,
But a shiny silk gown may become tattered and frayed.
A sweet juicy plum might meet its decay.
Even a walk in sunlight risks the scorching of rays.
But words—unlike these other simple things—
Words never ever go away.
So let me sit with you, if I may,
And tell you the warm thoughts I've been wanting to say.

The Final Barriers

You allowed the words to escape your lips—
the final barrier between intention and deed.
Did these gates first stop to think of repercussions?
Did they do their duty in the discussion?

Perhaps, deep down it was the mind
that forced the escape of the hidden motive.
Perhaps, deep down it was the soul
that permitted the final unfencing of the words of pain.
Whatever it was, those words will forever now remain.

One More Look

Take one more look
Within this book
Then tuck it on the shelf.
The words within
Will remain with you
They're a part now of yourself.

Return some day,
If you will,
To read from it again.
You'll have a new view, my friend.
It will be different then.

Then read it still
Just one more time
After some years have gone by,
And it will have changed even yet again,
And you will wonder why.

And I will say, it is not the book,
It is *you* who's not the same.
You've a keener eye and experience
To add now to your name.

So read it time-and-time again,
Let your thoughts become reflective.
And every time you reach the end,
You'll have a new perspective.

Send Me the Words of Peace

I have heard it said, that words can start a war.
Words said within steps of you, can wound someone afar.
They can send young soldiers off to war to be
    totally devoured.
They can ruin what is most sacred in this world of ours.

Words—just simple letters intertwined,
That can hold tremendous meaning when combined.
They can have invincible power when written upon the lines
And can freeze us in our tracks when blared
    across headlines.

But, is it possible that words
Can take us to a different place—
One where humanity will not be displaced?
A place where animosity can finally be replaced?
A place where our differences can finally be embraced?

Can we somehow create a time with one another,
Where there's finally no more harm
To our sisters and our brothers?
A time with no more broken fathers…
And no more crying mothers,
Just respect that is expressed for one another?

Send me the words to soothe our souls
That will conjure peace for young and old.
I want the words, that when they are told
Will allow a calmness to unfold.

I will not even add my name.
I am not seeking any fame.
It is not for *me* to be acclaimed.
I want only for **the words** to be proclaimed.

So please...
I sit here with my simple pen
And pray for those words to finally be sent.
I'll write each one down, you see, and then,
Release them to the world as I say, "Amen."

Peace

I Was Once Here

When I go away,
As we all must do,
May I leave a part of me with you?

May I leave my words
And thoughts behind,
For you to sometimes keep in mind?

May I leave my love
Upon these pages,
So that they may span across the ages?

Perhaps you'll find wisdom
Amongst the words,
Or encouragement
Within a verse.

Maybe you'll read them
From time-to-time
And tap to the rhythm
Or sway to the rhyme.

Or perhaps your soul may need fulfillment
And you'll find reading them is time well spent.

So if I leave my words—my gift—right here,
These thoughts I've shared that are so sincere,
Then even when I'm gone for many a year,
All will know...I was once here.

A Telling

They say I should have written
Years and years before,
But I wasn't ready yet.
I had to live a wee bit more.

It is life, you see,
That is upon these pages—
Experiences learned
Throughout various life stages.

Some were lived,
While others seen,
The rest all dwells
Somewhere between.

They were all summed up
And told through various words,
With meanings left
To be unfurled.

So embrace and reflect
Upon the joys and the strife,
Of the words on these pages
That reflect upon this life.

Remain up-to-date with the author:
Facebook: Clarise Annette Brooks—Author
Website: ClariseAnnetteBrooks.com
Instagram: ClariseAnnetteBrooks
Twitter: @Clarise_Writes